McAlpine

by Iain Gray

Lang**Syne**

PUBLISHING

WRITING *to* REMEMBER

79 Main Street, Newtongrange,
Midlothian EH22 4NA
Tel: 0131 344 0414
E-mail: info@lang-syne.co.uk
www.langsyneshop.co.uk

Design by Dorothy Meikle
Printed by Printwell Ltd
© Lang Syne Publishers Ltd 2024

All rights reserved. No part of this publication may be reproduced, stored or introduced into a retrieval system, or transmitted in any form or by any means (electronic, mechanical, photocopying, recording or otherwise) without the prior written permission of Lang Syne Publishers Ltd.

ISBN 978-1-85217-789-8

McAlpine

MOTTO:
Cuimhnich Bàs Ailpean
(Remember the Death of Alpin)

CRESTS include:
A boar's head
(and)
the severed head of a man

TERRITORY:
Argyll

NAME variations include:
MacAlpine
MacAlpin
McAlpin
MacAilpean

Chapter one:

The origins of the clan system

by Rennie McOwan

The original Scottish clans of the Highlands and the great families of the Lowlands and Borders were gatherings of families, relatives, allies and neighbours for mutual protection against rivals or invaders.

Scotland experienced invasion from the Vikings, the Romans and English armies from the south. The Norman invasion of what is now England also had an influence on land-holding in Scotland. Some of these invaders stayed on and in time became 'Scottish'.

The word clan derives from the Gaelic language term 'clann', meaning children, and it was first used many centuries ago as communities were formed around tribal lands in glens and mountain fastnesses.

The format of clans changed over the centuries, but at its best the chief and his family held the land on behalf of all, like trustees, and the ordinary clansmen and women believed they had a blood relationship with the founder of their clan.

There were two way duties and obligations. An inadequate chief could be deposed and replaced by someone of greater ability.

Clan people had an immense pride in race. Their relationship with the chief was like adult children to a father and they had a real dignity.

The concept of clanship is very old and a more feudal notion of authority gradually crept in.

Pictland, for instance, was divided into seven principalities ruled by feudal leaders who were the strongest and most charismatic leaders of their particular groups.

By the sixth century the 'British' kingdoms of Strathclyde, Lothian and Celtic Dalriada (Argyll) had emerged and Scotland, as one nation, began to take shape in the time of King Kenneth MacAlpin.

Some chiefs claimed descent from ancient kings which may not have been accurate in every case.

By the twelfth and thirteenth centuries the clans and families were more strongly brought under the central control of Scottish monarchs.

Lands were awarded and administered more and more under royal favour, yet the power of the area clan chiefs was still very great

The long wars to ensure Scotland's

independence against the expansionist ideas of English monarchs extended the influence of some clans and reduced the lands of others.

Those who supported Scotland's greatest king, Robert the Bruce, were awarded the territories of the families who had opposed his claim to the Scottish throne.

In the Scottish Borders country – the notorious Debatable Lands – the great families built up a ferocious reputation for providing warlike men accustomed to raiding into England and occasionally fighting one another.

Chiefs had the power to dispense justice and to confiscate lands and clan warfare produced a society where martial virtues – courage, hardiness, tenacity – were greatly admired.

Gradually the relationship between the clans and the Crown became strained as Scottish monarchs became more orientated to life in the Lowlands and, on occasion, towards England.

The Highland clans spoke a different language, Gaelic, whereas the language of Lowland Scotland and the court was Scots and in more modern times, English.

Highlanders dressed differently, had different

customs, and their wild mountain land sometimes seemed almost foreign to people living in the Lowlands.

It must be emphasised that Gaelic culture was very rich and story-telling, poetry, piping, the clarsach (harp) and other music all flourished and were greatly respected.

Highland culture was different from other parts of Scotland but it was not inferior or less sophisticated.

Central Government, whether in London or Edinburgh, sometimes saw the Gaelic clans as a challenge to their authority and some sent expeditions into the Highlands and west to crush the power of the Lords of the Isles.

Nevertheless, when the eighteenth century Jacobite Risings came along the cause of the Stuarts was mainly supported by Highland clans.

The word Jacobite comes from the Latin for James – Jacobus. The Jacobites wanted to restore the exiled Stuarts to the throne of Britain.

The monarchies of Scotland and England became one in 1603 when King James VI of Scotland (1st of England) gained the English throne after Queen Elizabeth died.

The Union of Parliaments of Scotland and England, the Treaty of Union, took place in 1707.

Some Highland clans, of course, and Lowland families opposed the Jacobites and supported the incoming Hanoverians.

After the Jacobite cause finally went down at Culloden in 1746 a kind of ethnic cleansing took place. The power of the chiefs was curtailed. Tartan and the pipes were banned in law.

Many emigrated, some because they wanted to, some because they were evicted by force. In addition, many Highlanders left for the cities of the south to seek work.

Many of the clan lands became home to sheep and deer shooting estates.

But the warlike traditions of the clans and the great Lowland and Border families lived on, with their descendants fighting bravely for freedom in two world wars.

Remember the men from whence you came, says the Gaelic proverb, and to that could be added the role of many heroic women.

The spirit of the clan, of having roots, whether Highland or Lowland, means much to thousands of people.

Meanwhile, many families proudly boast the heraldic device known as a Coat of Arms,.

The central motif of the Coat of Arms would originally have been what was sometimes borne on the shield of a warrior to distinguish himself from others on the battlefield.

Clan warfare produced a society where courage and tenacity were greatly admired

Chapter two:

The Seed of Alpin

A proud clan whose origins remain shrouded in the dim mists of time, the McAlpines – in spelling variants that include McAlpin, MacAlpine and MacAlpin – are recognised of being truly royal race.

With their early history frustratingly obscure, despite the efforts of scholars to tease out the tangled roots of their genesis and subsequent emergence into the clearer light of historical record, much is based on myth and clan tradition passed down over the ages.

A persistent tradition is that the McAlpines, more properly known in Gaelic as *MacAilpein*, indicating 'son of Alpin', are of royal blood through him.

This is why they, along with other clans the MacAulays, Macfies, Mackinnons, Macnabs, MacQuarries and Gregors (MacGregors), claim to be of the *Siol Alpin* – the Seed of Alpin.

But who was this character so central to the traditions of the Seed of Alpin?

In common with much of the McAlpine's

early history, there are a number of confusing and conflicting accounts.

A common theme, however, is that he was Alpin mac Echdach, a chieftain of royal Irish roots who was a ninth century king of Dál Riata.

Also known as Dál Riada or Dalriada, this Gaelic kingdom embraced the north-eastern part of the Emerald Isle and the western seaboard of Scotland, with the hillfort of Dunadd, in Argyll, its capital from about the sixth century.

A rocky crag that dominates the surrounding landscape, Dunadd is known for unique rock carvings and a mysterious 'footprint' in stone that is thought to have once formed part of an elaborate and long-forgotten ritual involving the succession of one king to another.

To place one's foot in the hollowed-out footprint may have represented the king's right to literally stamp his mark on the land on which he stood, by right of hereditary succession and battle-prowess.

Also of great ritual significance to the Dál Riatans was the site of what are now the ruins of Dunstaffnage Castle, known in Gaelic as *Caisteal Dhun Stadhainis*, built in the thirteenth century by the MacDougall lords of Lorn.

Located about three miles (5km) from Oban at the southwest entry to Loch Etive, this stronghold is where the Stone of Destiny, or *Lia Fail*, on which Scottish kings were enthroned for many centuries, is thought to have been kept after being brought from Ireland and then subsequently to Scone, in Perthshire.

It was the Dál Riatans, meanwhile, referred to by the Romans as *Scoti* – Scots – who gave their name to what we now know as 'Scotland.'

Returning to the McAlpine 'name-father' Alpin mac Echdach, he is said to have succeeded his father Eochaid as king in about 830.

According to the twelfth century *Cronica Regum Scottorum*, *The Chronicle of the Kings of Scots*, he was killed in battle against the Picts in Galloway, in the southwest of Scotland, four years later – either slain while fighting or beheaded after the battle.

The chronicle which, it must be stressed, is not wholly reliable, asserts Alpin's mother was the sister and heiress of Causantío mac Fergusa, King of the Picts, while he married a Dál Riatan (Scottish) princess.

This Pictish connection is important in attempting to understand the crucial events that followed in the wake of his succession by his son Coinneach mac Ailpean, also known as Cináed mac Ailpin, but more familiarly as Kenneth MacAlpin.

A powerful confederation of tribes, the Picts, or Picti, were so-named by the Romans to describe 'painted or tattooed people' and are thought to have been descendants of tribes including the Caledonii.

It would appear that, through the Pictish system of matrilinear succession, Kenneth, born in 810, became not only 'King of Scots' on the death of his father but also 'King of Picts.'

This potent fusion of both royal houses under Kenneth led to the creation of the Kingdom of Alba, later the Kingdom of Scotland, in about 850.

Some sources claim this came about through both kingdoms combining their strengths to repel the increasing threat from Viking incursions.

This appears plausible – although there are other more lurid accounts that he achieved the union through guile and force of arms.

The medieval *The Prophecy of Berchan* asserts that, beset by Pictish rivals, Kenneth invited seven of them and their entourages to a lavish banquet at Scone.

In what is known as 'MacAlpin's Treason',

the Gaels of Dalriada, against the rules of hospitality and at MacAlpin's behest, came armed to the feast.

Plied with copious amounts of fiery alcohol, the Picts became almost senseless and the Gaels then pulled bolts from the benches on which they sat – tumbling them into a concealed pit bristling with sharp blades on which they were impaled.

The remainder of the Pictish entourage,

Some sources claim that both kingdoms combined their strengths to repel the increasing threat from Viking incursions.

according to this gruesome account, were then slaughtered to a man and MacAlpin emerged as ruler over all he surveyed.

But by whatever means he achieved his aims, he is nevertheless regarded as having united the kingdoms and, as Kenneth I, recognised as the first king of the unified Kingdom of Scotland.

He died in 858, reportedly from a tumour while, his legend living on, he acquired the posthumous nickname *An Ferbasach* – The Conqueror – and at least two of his sons, Áed and Constantine, succeeding him as kings.

To this day the McAlpine/MacAlpine name is found in significant numbers in the Kilmartin area of their original heartland of Argyll while, despite their distinguished descent from the first King of Scots, at the moment they have no Hereditary Chief.

But this may change within the next few years.

On September 10, 2016, a rather unusual gathering took place in the magnificent setting of Abbotsford House, in the Borders, home of the great antiquarian and novelist Sir Walter Scott.

In a bid for formal recognition to some degree of their ancient heritage, the international

Clan MacAlpine Society held a Derbhfine, or Family Convention, to select and recommend Michael Todd McAlpin, Snr; for the role of Commander of MacAlpine.

This was formally recognised by Dr Joseph Morrow, Lord Lyon King of Arms of Scotland, on April 19, 2017, and the society commented how this "has empowered him (Michael Todd McAlpin) to do and perform all acts and functions proper for a period of ten years or until a chief is named."

Should a chief be so named, this would give official recognition for a Chiefly Coat of Arms and related crest.

Although the motto *Cuimhnich Bàs Ailpean – Remember the Death of Alpin –* has for many centuries been the clan's recognised motto, there has been no single, official crest.

A previous Lord Lyon King of Arms, however, Sir Thomas Innes of Learney, stated that the ancient crest was a boar's head within a royal or antique crown.

Other crests, meanwhile, include the severed head of a man – with reference to the beheading of the clan's 'name-father' Alpin mac Echdach, and this is the one we feature.

Chapter three:

McAlpine's Fusiliers

One Scottish dynasty of the McAlpine name have left an enduring legacy on the landscape in the form of major construction works that range from an iconic railway viaduct, dams and roads to an exhibition centre and the stadium for the 2012 London Olympics.

The beginnings of what is known today as the construction company Sir Robert McAlpine stretch back to 1847 with the birth in the small North Lanarkshire village of Newarthill of the pioneering civil engineer and entrepreneur from whom the enterprise takes its name.

Leaving school when aged ten to work in a coalmine and later apprenticed as a bricklayer, his skills and commercial acumen were such that he was able to embark in the construction business in his own right, working on early projects that included the Singer Sewing Machine factory in Clydebank and some of the tunnelling work for the Glasgow Subway.

But the project for which he is most noted is the renowned Glenfinnan Viaduct.

Standing 100ft (30.48m) above the River Finnan on the West Highland railway line in Inverness-shire, connecting Fort William and Mallaig and at the top of Loch Shiel, work on the viaduct began in 1896 and completed only two years later.

Living up to his nickname 'Concrete Bob', McAlpine used mass concrete in its construction – a technique he pioneered in favour of reinforced concrete and which is formed by pouring concrete, usually using fine aggregate, into what is known as 'formwork'.

At 416 yards (380m) the longest concrete railway bridge in Scotland and built on a curve of 792ft (241m), it is famously traversed by the Hogwarts Express steam train in the *Harry Potter* series of films.

A popular visitor attraction, during the summer the heritage Jacobite steam train plies its route while it has also been a location for other films and television series including *The Crown* and *Monarch of the Glen*.

Made a baronet in 1918 as Sir Robert McAlpine, 1st Baronet, 'Concrete Bob' died in 1934.

Through his first marriage to Agnes Hepburn, who died in 1888, he was the father of two daughters, Agnes and Ethel and five sons Robert, William,

Thomas (better known by his middle name Malcolm), Alfred and Granville.

Another son, Archibald Douglas McAlpine and two daughters were born through his second marriage in 1889 to Florence Palmer.

It was through the company then known as Robert McAlpine and Sons that work on the Glenfinnan Viaduct was carried out – with his third eldest son Malcolm acting as his assistant and oldest son Robert in charge of construction.

Born in 1877 and the recipient in later years of a knighthood, Sir Malcolm McAlpine was responsible for the idea of using water under high pressure, rather than steam pressure, to power drilling operations on particularly hard rock.

The rather unlikely setting for this 'Eureka' moment was at his dentist, when he saw how his drill for fillings used water pressure.

Massively scaling this up, it was utilised in a wide range of projects including the dam across Loch Dubh, in the West Highlands.

Severely injured in a blasting operation, he recovered and, during the First World War, was in charge of the construction of a huge motor transport depot at Slough, Berkshire, for the War Office.

During the next war, he oversaw construction of the ingenuous Mulberry Harbours – the large concrete units towed across the Channel to form vital breakwaters as artificial harbours for the D-Day landings at Normandy.

In more peaceful pursuits before the war, he also supervised the construction of Wembley Stadium, home of English football, and the building of his family-owned Dorchester Hotel, London.

Having been appointed chairman of McAlpines in 1951, he died in 1967.

Set to a traditional Irish air, meanwhile, the rousing ballad *McAlpine's Fusiliers* recalls the hard toil of the vast army of men who laboured on some of the company's most dirty and dangerous projects such as dams and tunnels.

Known as 'navvies', they were drawn from all parts, but particularly Ireland.

With the words attributed to the late Irish writer and musician Dominic Behan and recorded by bands including the Clancy Brothers and the Dubliners, one typical verse is:

I've worked till the sweat near had me beat
with Russian, Czech and Pole,
At shuttering jams up in the hydro dams, or

> *underneath the Thames in a hole,*
> *I grafted hard and I got me cards and many*
> *a ganger's fist across my ears.*
> *If you pride your life, don't join, by Christ,*
> *with McAlpine's Fusiliers.*

In contemporary times, working conditions for those employed as 'McAlpine Fusiliers' are decidedly much improved.

Showcase projects they have toiled on in recent years include The Millennium Dome, now known as The O2 Arena, on the Greenwich peninsula, southeast London.

The ninth largest building in the world by usable volume and opened in 2000 to house the Millennium Experience exhibition, the stunning structure was constructed as a joint venture between the companies Sir Robert McAlpine and Laing Management.

Sir Robert McAlpine was also the main contractor for yet another prestigious London facility – the magnificent stadium built in the Stratford district of the city to host track and field events for the 2012 Olympics.

Now known as the London Stadium, it also serves as home to West Ham United football club.

Returning to the early years of the McAlpine dynasty, Sir Alfred David McAlpine, born in 1881, and the fourth oldest son of Sir Robert, 1st baronet, formed the company's offshoot Sir Alfred McAlpine and Son, which confined itself to work in the north-west of England.

He died in 1944, while he was the father of Alfred James "Jimmie" McAlpine, born in 1908, and who took over chairmanship of the company.

Residing at Gerwyn Hall in the village of Marchwiel, near Wrexham, Denbighshire, in North Wales and a keen cricketer as his father had been, he was also noted for his valuable car collection that included models from Jaguar, Rolls-Royce, Bentley, Aston Martin and Bugatti.

He died in 1991, while he was a nephew of a member of the family dynasty who found fame not in the construction industry but in medicine.

This was Archibald Douglas McAlpine, born in 1890 and the son of Sir Robert McAlpine, 1st Baronet, through his second marriage.

A neurologist and pioneering researcher into multiple sclerosis, he graduated from Glasgow University in 1913 with degrees in both medicine and surgery and served during the First World War firstly in the Royal Army Medical Corps (RAMC) and then as a surgeon-lieutenant in the Royal Navy.

Appointed neurologist to the Middlesex Hospital in 1923 and, during the Second World War, as a brigadier in the RAMC, he later became a leading expert in the study of multiple sclerosis.

Instrumental in the formation in 1953 of the Multiple Sclerosis Society of Great Britain, his ground-breaking work *Multiple Sclerosis*, first published in 1955 and reprinted a number of times since as *McAlpine's Multiple Sclerosis*, remains one of the most authoritative of its kind on the condition.

Also responsible for pioneering work on organic mercury poisoning and a member of the Royal College of Physicians, London, he died in 1981.

One distinguished member of the McAlpine dynasty who was nevertheless the subject of wholly unwarranted controversy in the latter years of his life was the businessman, art collector and Conservative Party politician Robert Alistair McAlpine, more formally known as Lord McAlpine.

Born in 1942 and a great-grandson of the founder of the family dynasty Sir Robert McAlpine, he was made a director of its construction business when aged 21, while he also worked for a time as a property developer in Australia.

Appointed treasurer of the Conservative Party in 1975 by future Prime Minister Margaret Thatcher, then the leader of the party, a post he held until 1990, his personal political views ranged from scepticism over membership of the EU and support for the decriminalisation of all drugs.

Created a life peer as Baron McAlpine of West Green, of West Green in the County of Hampshire in 1984, he was expelled from the Conservative Party in 1997 after joining the Referendum Party, later becoming its leader and, after it became defunct, rejoining his old party.

In November of 2012 he was falsely implicated in a North Wales child abuse scandal when a BBC Newsnight programme accused an unnamed "senior Conservative" of abuse. Social media wildly speculated from this that the person referred to was Lord McAlpine – but it transpired he was in fact the victim of a case of mistaken identity.

It led to the BBC awarding him £185,000 in damages plus costs – which he donated to charity – and the resignation of the corporation's then director-general, with damages also won from ITV.

He died in 2014 while, far removed from politics and controversy, he had been a collector of art, modern sculpture and ephemera – at one stage owning a warehouse in which to store them and periodically donating some to art institutions.

Returning to politics and in the original McAlpine heartland of Scotland, Thomas McAlpine, better known as Tom McAlpine, was the Scottish National Party (SNP) politician born in 1929 in Wishaw, North Lanarkshire.

A founder member of the Scottish Campaign for Nuclear Disarmament (SCND) and a member of the Labour Party before joining the SNP in 1967, he died in 2006.

In contemporary nationalist politics, Joan McAlpine is the journalist and MSP (Member of the Scottish Parliament) who has represented the SNP for the South of Scotland region since 2011.

Born in 1962 in Gourock, Renfrewshire and formerly married to the musician and writer Pat Kane of the pop duo Hue and Cry, newspapers she has worked for include the *Scotsman*, the *Sunday Times Scotland*, where she served as editor in 2000, and later the *Herald* as deputy editor – the first woman to hold the post.

Chapter four:

On the world stage

Bearers of the McAlpine name and its popular spelling variants have achieved recognition through a diverse range of endeavours and pursuits.

Behind the camera lens, **Donald McAlpine** is the award-winning Australian cinematographer born in 1934 in Quandialia, New South Wales.

Films he has worked on include the 1972 *The Adventures of Barry McKenzie*, the 1976 *Don's Party* and, from 1980, *Breaker Morant*, while he was nominated for an Academy Award for the 2001 *Moulin Rouge!*

A member of the Australian Cinematographers Society (ACS) and the American Society of Cinematographers (ASC), he was honoured by the latter with its 2009 International Achievement Award.

On British television screens **Jennie McAlpine** is the actress and comedian known for her role since 2001 of Fiz Brown in the popular soap *Coronation Street*.

Born in 1984 in Bury, Greater Manchester

and the winner when she was aged 13 of a Young Comedian of the Year Competition run by a soft drink brand, she also played the role from 1999 to 2000 of Michelle Morley in the soap *Emmerdale*.

In the world of music, **William McAlpine** was the noted Scottish tenor born in 1922 in Stenhousemuir, Falkirk.

His beginnings were humble – he worked as a bricklayer before his talent was spotted and he was encouraged to study at the Guildhall School of Music, London.

Making his stage debut in 1951 in a Royal Opera House production of Richard Strauss's *Salome*, he joined the Sadlers Wells Company in 1956 as principal tenor.

Later singing with Glyndebourne Festival Opera and Scottish Opera, after retiring from the stage he returned to his old alma mater the Guildhall School of Music, where he taught up until his death in 2004.

Born in 1870, the son of a Leicester clothier, **Colin McAlpin** was the prolific English composer of operas, ballet music and songs whose first composition, *The Cuckoo*, was performed at his local school when he was aged only 15.

Having studied both harmony and organ

playing at the Royal Academy of Music, London and winning awards in both disciplines, his opera in three acts *Robin Hood* was performed at the Leicester Philharmonic Society in 1897.

His acclaimed *The Cross and the Crescent* was first produced at Covent Garden in 1903, winning him the prestigious Manners Prize for best opera by a British composer.

Also a highly respected critical essayist for journals including *Musical Times* and *Musical Quarterly*, he died in 1942.

In contemporary music and a much different genre, **Tony MacAlpine** is the American rock solo guitarist and composer born in 1960 in Springfield, Massachusetts.

Starting to play piano when aged five and picking up the guitar when aged twelve, he studied violin and classical piano at the Springfield Conservatory of Music in his home state before embarking on a career in rock.

Albums include the 1986 *Edge of Insanity* and the 2015 *Concrete Gardens*, while he has also played with the heavy metal super group M.A.R.S. and on keyboards on albums by fellow guitarists Joey Tafolla and Vinnie Moore.

Bearers of the McAlpine name have also excelled in the highly competitive world of sport.

On the motor racing track, **Kenneth McAlpine**, a great-grandson of Sir Robert McAlpine, founder of the civil engineering business of the name, is the British former driver and wine business entrepreneur who participated in seven Formula One World Championship Grand Prix, starting with his first race in 1952.

Born in 1920 in Cobham, Surrey, after his driving career ended he contributed to the sport through his financial backing of the Connaught Racing Team.

When the team broke up in 1958 – and a number of its cars sold to a then relatively unknown Bernie Ecclestone, former chief executive of the Formula One Group which manages Formula One – he set up an English wine growing and bottling business at his estate in Lamberhurst, Kent.

In the rough and tumble of rugby union, **Rob McAlpine** is the Scottish player who was the recipient of a Scotland Club XV cap in 2016.

Born in 1991, clubs he has played for include Edinburgh Rugby, Glasgow Warriors and Ayr RFC.

From rugby to the football pitch, James Barbour McAlpine, better known as **J.B. McAlpine** or by his nickname Mutt McAlpine, was the Scottish amateur inside left noted for his career in the Scottish League with Glasgow club Queen's Park.

Born in 1901 and the club's record scorer – having netted 192 goals in 547 appearances – he later served as its president.

He died in 1975, while in 2013 the club named its new youth and community building at Lesser Hampden the J.B. McAlpine Pavilion in his honour.

Selected as Scottish Football Writers' Association (SWFA) Footballer of the Year in 1985, **Hamish McAlpine** is the retired goalkeeper born in 1948 in Kilspindie, Perth and Kinross.

With Dundee United from 1966 to 1986 and having represented his nation at under-21 level, other teams he played for include Raith Rovers and Arbroath.

From sport to the world of journalism, **Harry S. McAlpin** broke down an American racial barrier in 1944 when he became the first African-American reporter allowed to cover a White House press conference.

Born in 1906 in St Louis, Missouri, after studying journalism and advertising at the University of Wisconsin he worked from 1926 to 1929 as a reporter, editor and office manager for the African-American newspaper the *Washington Tribune*.

Also qualifying as a lawyer and working for a number of bodies representing the interests of African-Americans in addition to reporting for the *Chicago Defender*, the body then known as the National Negro Publishers Association (NNPA) petitioned the White House Correspondents Association (WHCA) for him to be granted press credentials.

It took some months for the association to agree but eventually, on February 8, 1944, he made White House history by attending his first U.S. Presidential news conference – with President Franklin D. Roosevelt warmly shaking his hand and saying: "I'm glad to see you, McAlpin, and very happy you are here."

Later moving to Louisville, Kentucky, he served there until 1953 as the only African-American assistant commonwealth attorney.

He died in 1985, while in 2014 he was posthumously honoured by the WHCA through the creation of a scholarship in his name and President Barack Obama praising his pioneering journalism.

One bearer of the McAlpine name with a rather unusual claim to fame is the American science journalist Katherine McAlpine, better known as **Kate McAlpine**.

Born in 1985 in Cedar Rapids, Iowa and the holder of dual degrees in physics and professional writing from Michigan State University, she writes on scientific matters for publications including *New Scientist* and *ScienceNow*.

But in 2008 she hit upon another decidedly more novel way of explaining some of the deep mysteries of science.

This is through the music genre of rap – the idea first coming to her while working in 2008 at CERN (European Organisation for Nuclear Research), in Switzerland.

As scientists tried their best to enlighten the layperson to the mysteries of subjects such as the particle accelerator known as the Large Hydron Collider, McAlpine did so in rap terms.

This was through the YouTube video *Large Hadron Rap*, complete with dancers and music by Will Barras, which she wrote, produced and performed under the pseudonym 'alpinecat'.

The video became a viral hit, while equally popular rap videos explaining the nature of the universe include *Black Hole Rap* and *Rare Isotope Rap*.